Sequoyah

THE CHEROKEE MAN WHO GAVE HIS PEOPLE WRITING
ᏍᏏᏉᏯ ᎠᏍᎦᏯ ᏓᎵᎦ ᎤᏣᏥ ᏗᎦᏪ ᏎᎾ ᏅᎩᏌᏱᏛᏗ

by James Rumford

Houghton Mifflin Company Boston

Translated into Cherokee by Anna Sixkiller Huckaby,
with the author's deep appreciation.

Copyright © 2004 by James Rumford

All rights reserved. For information about permission
to reproduce selections from this book, write to Permissions,
Houghton Mifflin Company, 215 Park Avenue South, New York, New York 10003.

The illustrations were done with ink, watercolor, pastel, and pencil on drawing paper
adhered to a rough piece of wood, the texture of which was brought out with each pass
of chalk and colored pencil. To solve the complex issues of color and composition in
"tall" pictures, the author turned to the works of the Navajo Quincy Tahoma (1920–1956),
the contemporary Chinese artist He Jiaying (b. 1957), and the Japanese woodcut master
Hiroshige (1797–1858) for inspiration.

The English translation of the Cherokee words in the illustrations:
[pg. 7] Sequoia tree; [pg. 10] spoons and forks; [pg. 14] Sequoyah working;
[pg. 16] troublemakers; [pg. 18] fire; [pg. 20] Ayoka and Sequoyah; [pg. 22]
Sequoyah and the first letters; [pg. 26] the first line of "Amazing Grace,"
a favorite hymn of the Cherokee.

www.houghtonmifflinbooks.com

The text of this book is set in Walbaum .

Library of Congress Cataloging-in-Publication Data
Rumford, James, 1948–
    Sequoyah : the man who gave his people writing / by James Rumford.
        p. cm.
    ISBN 0-618-36947-3
    1. Sequoyah, 1770?–1843. 2. Cherokee Indians—Biography. 3. Cherokee language—
Writing. 4. Cherokee language—Alphabet. I. Title.
    E99.C5S3875 2004
    975.004'97557'0092—dc22

                                    2004000980

Printed in Malaysia
TWP 10 9
4500350737

To my father,
Sydney Rumford,
who would stop
the car to read
every historic
marker and who
would certainly
have told us
this story.

California, 1958.

Look at the tall trees, says my father.

They are redwood trees. They have been alive for thousands of years.

They are called the Giant Sequoia.

Where did the name come from?

It came from the name of a Cherokee Indian man who was alive when the United States was new.

ᏗᏣᎧᏅᎦ ᎢᎾ ᎢᏗᎦᎳ ᏕᏡᎬᎢ, ᎠᏗᎭ ᎡᏙᏓ.

ᎩᎦᎨᏃ ᎠᏓ ᏂᏕᏡᎦ. ᎠᎴ ᏌᏊ ᏯᎦᏴᎵ ᎾᏕᏗᏯ ᏥᏗᏡᎪᎢ.

ᏧᎳᎾ ᏍᏏᏉᏯ ᏓᏃᏎᎨᎢ.

ᎭᏢᏃ ᏧᏓᎴᏁ ᎯᎠ ᏂᏚᏙᎠ?

ᎠᏣᎳᎩᏃ ᎠᏍᎦᏯ ᎠᎴ ᏁᏙᎲ ᎠᎹᏰᏟ ᎢᏳ ᏂᎨᎭ ᎾᎾᏃ ᏧᏓᎴᏁ.

This Sequoyah must have been famous, we say.

He must have fought bravely and led his people well.

He must have been as tall and as strong as these trees.

Yes, my father says, but not as you might think.

ᎦᏔ ᎥᏆᎤᏯ ᎠᏯᏍᏯ ᎤᎵᏯᏈᎵ ᎨᏎ, ᏝᏗᏈ.

ᏗᏟᎤᏯᏛ ᎤᏢᏫ ᎷᏛᏁ ᏛᎥᏈ ᎠᎭᏴᎧ.

ᎤᏯᏭᏯ ᎦᏔ ᏔᎧ ᏛᏗᏛ ᏍᏫᎬ ᏛᎰᏴᎵ.

ᎥᎥ, ᎤᏯᎩ ᎭᏍᏲᏯᎬ ᎡᎳᎵ, Ꭲ ᏯᎩ ᎬᎶᎤᏛ.

This man called Sequoyah was crippled.

He was born in eastern Tennessee in the 1760s, the son of a Cherokee woman and a white man he never knew.

For much of his life, Sequoyah was nobody famous.

He was a metalworker who could turn iron into chisels and drills and Georgia silver into forks and spoons.

ᎯᎢᎾ ᎠᏍᎦᏯ ᏍᏏᏉᏯ ᎠᏲᎤᏣ ᎨᏎᎢ.

ᎤᏕᏅᏃ ᏭᏕᎬᎢᏗᏟ ᏖᎾᏏ ᎦᎵᏆᏚᎢᏍᎪᎯᏧᏈ ᏑᏓᎵᏍᎪᎯ ᎤᏕᏘᏴᏌᏗᏒ, ᎤᏥᏃ ᎠᎶᎳᎩ ᎠᎴ ᎤᏙᏓ ᎠᏲᏣᏁᎦ Ꮭ ᎪᎵᎩ ᏱᎨᏎ.

ᏍᏏᏉᏯ ᎪᎯᏗ ᎤᎴᏂᏙᎴ Ꮭ ᏧᏓᏃᎶᎵ ᏱᎨᏎ.

ᏔᎷᎩᏍᎩ ᎦᏅᎦᏟᎶᏍᎩ ᎨᏎ ᏗᎦᏁᎦᎳᏫᏍᏙᏗ ᎠᎴ ᏗᏔᎴᏍᏙᏗ ᏕᎪᎵᏍᎬ. Georgia ᎠᏕᎳ ᎤᏁᎦ ᏗᏗᏙᏗ ᎠᎴ ᏰᎩ ᏕᎪᎵᏗᏍᎬ.

Sequoyah was not a chief, but he loved his people like one.

He wanted them to stand as tall as any people on earth.

He did not want them to disappear in the white man's world.

He did not want their Cherokee voices to fade away.

ᏎᏉᏯᎾᏃ Ꮃ ᎤᎬᏫᎠᎦᏙ ᎦᎥᏎ ᎠᏓᎨᏴᏂ ᏍᏲᏥᏒ ᏧᏫᏪ ᎠᏂᏴᏫ ᏁᎠᏴᎠ ᎤᎬᏫᎠᎦᏙ ᎨᏒᎢ.

ᎤᏍᏕᎠᎬ ᏔᏁ ᏔᎵᏴᏗ ᏧᏴᏩᏗ ᏁᎠᏴᎠ ᏁᏂ ᏴᏁ ᏣᎦᏙ ᎠᏅᎮ.

Ꮃ ᎦᏍᎮᎠᏋ ᎤᏁᏢᎢᏙᏗ ᏁᎠᏴᎠ ᎠᏂᏟᏁᏍ ᏔᎦᏁᎮᏢᏙᏗ.

Ꮃ ᎦᏍᎮᎠᏋ ᎦᏬᏯ ᏔᏗᏁ ᎤᎠᎭᏃᎠᏗ.

When he was fifty, they say, he decided to capture the people's voices in writing.

But Sequoyah, they tell us, knew no English and couldn't read—not even the letter A.

But that didn't matter to Sequoyah.

"I will invent writing for our people," he said.

Everyone laughed.

"Writing will make us strong."

No one believed him.

ᏏᏲᎠᏏ ᏓᏍᎫᏞ ᎭᏚᏀ, ᎠᎾᏏᏪᎬ, ᏎᏲᎠᏫᎤ ᏣᏂᏋᏗ ᎠᏲ ᏣᎤᏑᎫᏗ ᏔᏧᎴᎮᏏᎬ.

ᎠᏘᏃ ᏏᏅᎣᏪ, ᎠᎾᏏᏪᎠ, Ꮅ ᎠᏊᏣᏍ ᎠᎿᏍ ᎠᏲ ᎠᎠᏞᏛᏏᏲ ᏐᎭᏞ ᎵᏪᏫ ᎠᏲ ᏥᎵᎫᎮᏪᎬ ᎠᏊᏣᏍ ᏆᎠᎿᏗ.

ᎠᏘᏃ Ꮅ ᎾᏫᏲᎾ ᏓᏣᎤᎵᏭᏝ ᏏᏅᎣᏪ.

"ᎶᎭᏟᎤᎮᏏ ᏔᏣᎾᏗ ᏨᎠᏫᎫᏗ ᎠᏫ ᎢᏲᏧᏪ ᏔᏣᏐᎾ," ᎤᎱᏝᎢ.

ᎮᏍᏗᏃ ᎬᏣᏋᏪᏝ.

"ᏐᏗᏫᏫᏈ ᎤᏟᎲᏲᏞ ᏍᎭᎵᏍ."

Ꮅ ᏲᏓ ᎭᏟ ᏈᏈᏅᏗ.

Sequoyah began drawing hundreds of symbols,
one for each word.

He scratched them on slats of wood and filled his
cabin with shingles of writing.

ᎪᏴᎢᏔᏃ ᎤᏍᏣᏖ ᏤᏨᏭᎡ ᏞᎬᏨᎥᏗ ᏁᎯᏢᏭ ᏩᏫᎩ
ᏚᎤᏂᏲᏭᏗ, ᎻᏬ ᏤᎬᏭᏗ ᎻᏬ ᎢᎯᏢᏭᏗ.

ᏣᏝᏫᎩᏃ ᏞᎬᏭᏖᏗ ᏁᎯᏢᏭᏗ ᎠᏘ ᏍᎨᎧᏚ ᎤᎤᎮᏒ ᏣᎤᏮᏫᎤ.

"He is crazy," the people jeered. They feared his signs were evil.

"We should teach him a lesson," the neighbors hooted. They saw no use for writing.

"Let's burn down his cabin," they cried. "We have to make him stop."

"ᎸᏓᏅᏛᎾᏛ," ᎠᎾᏗᏍᎨ ᎠᏂᏴᏫ. ᏓᏂᏍᎦᎢᎯ ᏧᏣᏩᏍᏔᏅ ᎠᎴ ᏧᏬᏪᏔᏅ ᎤᏐᏅᎢᏃ ᎠᏁᎵᏍᎨ ᎸᏍᏛ ᏚᏣᏩᏍᏛ ᎠᎴ ᏚᏬᏪᎸ.

"ᎡᏕᏲᎲᎦ ᎯᎠ ᎤᏓᏅᏕᏙᏗ," ᎠᎾᏗᏍᎨ ᎾᎥ ᎢᏳᎾᏓᎵ. ᏝᏃ ᎪᎨᏍᏗ ᏗᎬᏙᏗ ᏱᎦᎩ ᎯᎠ ᏥᏚᏣᏩᏍᏗ ᎠᎴ ᏥᏚᏬᏪᎳ.

"ᎢᏓᎪᎲᏍᏗ ᎤᏓᏁᎸᎢ," ᎠᏏᎯᏅ. "ᎡᏓᎴᏫᏍᏙᏙᏗ ᎠᎾᏗᏍᎨᎢ."

So they burned his cabin down and turned his writing into smoke.

But Sequoyah learned a different lesson.

Sometimes disaster happens for a reason. Sometimes it says: "Follow a different path."

ᏏᏲᏃ ᏅᏔᎠᏓᎤᏯᎵ ᎤᏟᏝ ᎠᏕ ᎲᏍᏖ ᏙᎦᎾᏍᎸᏝ ᏙᏫᏆᏫᏅ ᏎᎸᎵ.

ᎠᎢᏃ ᏍᏰᏛᎤ ᎤᏍᏪᏍ ᎦᏎ ᏔᏩᏝᎵᎢ.

ᏔᏋᏔᏃ ᎠᎢᏬᏓ ᏃᎣᏴ ᎲᏎᎮᏮᏓᏍᎪ, ᎦᏎ ᏔᏎᏮᏝᏓ ᎠᏃᎦᏔᏔ.

Sequoyah, they say, gave up drawing a different symbol for each word. There were just too many marks and squiggles for anyone to remember.

Instead, they tell us, he invented letters to spell out the sounds of the language.

When he had enough letters—about eighty-four or so—he began writing.

His neighbors stopped laughing when Sequoyah's six-year-old daughter, Ayoka, learned to read.

The people stopped jeering when two warriors wrote to each other.

ᏆᏏᏴᎤᏃ ᏚᏞᏓᏔ ᏣᏌᏫᏈᏫᏈ ᏠᏯᏁᏔᏫᏗ ᎣᏌᏫᏴᏃ ᎨᏔ
ᏠᏯᏁᏔᏫᏗ ᎴᏲ ᎣᏌᏴᎤ ᏠᏟᎵᏗᏫᏗ ᎨᏔᎢ.

ᏃᏫᏃ ᎣᏲᏔᏲ ᏎᏃᏴᎬ ᏠᏯᏁᏔᏫᏗ ᏣᏌᏫᏈᏫᎬ ᏗᏆ ᏔᏴᎣᎮᏘᏫᏗ
ᎬᏔᎩ.

ᏰᏈᏫᏃ ᏔᏎ ᏎᏃᏴᎬ ᏎᏫᏫᏌᏫᎬ ᏫᏍᎲ ᏁᏈᏫᎪ ᎣᎩ ᎣᏲᏔᏲ
ᏣᏌᏫᏈᎬ ᏠᏯᏁᏔᏫᏗ ᎬᏔᎩ ᏎᏫᎮᏘᏫᏗ.

ᏅᎢᏃ ᏔᎬᏏᎵᏈ ᏫᎲᏲᏈᏏᎢ ᏫᎲᏰᎬᏫᎬ ᏅᎴᏈᏫᏴᎴᏫᏈ ᏆᏏᏴᏫ
ᎣᏫᎭ ᏲᎵᏈ ᏔᎬᏍᎴᏔᎵ ᎴᏓᎬᎬ ᎣᏍᎬᎢᏃ ᎴᏗᏒᎴᎩ ᎬᏔᎩ ᎴᏲ
ᏠᏫᏫᎬᎴᎩ.

ᏗᎲᏔᎴᏃ ᏫᎲᏲᏈᏏᎢ ᏗᏫᏴᏈᏘᏫᎬ Ᏸ ᏗᎲᏫᏈ ᏠᎴᏟᏓ ᎣᏰᏲᏟᏓ
ᏞᎴᏞᏴᏫᏮᏁᎦ ᎴᏲ ᏗᎲᏗᏈᏰᏫᎬ ᎬᏔᎩ.

ᏍᏅᎨ Ꭴ

A - YO - KA

This is how Sequoyah wrote Ayoka's name.

The people, they say, learned the Cherokee letters quickly.

Mothers and fathers, brothers and sisters left notes around the house so that they could teach each other to read.

People took trips so they could have the fun of writing letters and sending them back home.

It was not long, they tell us, before everyone was reading and writing.

The Cherokee Nation praised the writing Sequoyah invented.

And in 1824, they gave Sequoyah a silver medal.

DӨꝆꙍAZ DhBӨ ꝺCꙍꝆ ꝺӨSGᏆꝛ GWY ꝺZꙍGꝆ.

ꝆӨꝆꞰ, ꝆӨꝆVꝆ, DӨCꝺP Dꝺ ꝆӨꝆꝭ ꝺӨꝺꝺꝉ ꝆӨꝆVꙍWꞰꙍ AꙍP Dꝺ SꝼKS TꝭP ꝆhꝼꙍꞰ ꝆhAꝼBꝆ DBꝭꝉ Dꝺ ꝆӨꝆSꞀꙍꙍꞰ ꝆhAꝼBꝆT DhBӨZ ꝺӨꝺꝺꝉ TӨ ꝆꝆꞰ AꙍP ꝆӨꝆVꙍWӨꝆ ꝺhBꝭꝉ.

ꝆZ TGꙍꝭV hSꝆ GWY ꝆhAꝼBꙍꙍY ꝭꝼꙍWꞀ.

GWY DBꝼ ꝺꝼꝼꝼV ꙍbꝮꙍ SCMꝪꝮꙍ ꝆAꙍGꝆ GWY.

ꞀWS TꙍAꝭꝆꝮ WꝼꙍAꝭ ꝺY ꝆSꝆBꞀꝆꝛ DꞀꙆꝺ ꙍbꝮꙍ DSW ꝺꞀS DꝺꞀꙍꝆ.

This is how Sequoyah wrote his own name.

S - SI - QUO - YA

A missionary named Worcester helped Sequoyah turn his beautiful loops and spirals into sturdy, English-looking symbols that could be printed with lead type.

With these new signs, the Cherokee Nation published newspapers and books and made sure that their words would never fade away.

DⱤGVhⱦ Worcester ᒍVᎩᏓ ᎧⱲᏚᏆᏛ ⱲᏏᏙᎥⱲ ᎫᏚᏞᏟᏓⱲᎫ ᏚᎠⱲᏋ
ᎢᏚⱡ ᎤⱲᎩ ᎠⱲᎮ ᎫᏚᏯᏙᒍ ᎡᎮⱲ ᎫᎬᎻᎯᏯᏙᒍ ᎢᎬᎮⱲᏙᒍ.

ᏬᎢᏃ ᒍᏙ ᏚᎤᏯᎡ ᏃⱲ ᏩᎩ ᎠᏰᎮ ᎡᎮⱲ ᎫᎠⱲᎮ ᏚᎮᎯᏙᏰᎤ ᏬᏓ ᏩᎩ
ᒍᎡᎠᏞᏯᒍ ᎠᎧ ᏎⱲᎠᏆⱲᒍ ᎯⱦᎡᎤ.

	became	
A - YO - KA		A - YO - KA
S - SI - QUO - YA		S - SI - QUO - YA

ᏬᎥᏗᎣᎠ ᏬᏫᏂᎧ

Even when soldiers forced the people from their lands and sent them west in the 1830s, the Cherokee held on to their books.

Even when sickness half emptied their towns, they kept their writing.

Even when English-speaking teachers ruled their classrooms, long after Sequoyah had passed away, they remembered their letters. They never let them disappear.

ᎠᏂᏲᏍᎩ ᏧᎾᎴᏅᎯ ᏓᏂᏍᎳᏫᏗᏍᎬ ᎠᏂᏣᎳᎩ ᏚᏁᏅᎡ ᎠᎴ ᎦᏓ ᏚᏂᎲ ᏚᏂᎯᏰᎢ ᎠᏎ ᎤᎾᏓᏅᏍᏗ ᏥᏄᎵᏍᏔᏁ ᏁᎳᏚᎢᏍᎪᎯᏧᏈ ᏦᏍᎪᎯ ᎤᏕᏘᏴᏌᏗᏒ ᎨᏒᎢ. ᎠᎴ ᎪᏪᎵ ᏧᏃᏪᎳᏅ ᏚᏂᎾᏫᏛᎮ.

ᎠᎴᏍᏊ ᎢᏳᎩ ᎬᏗ ᎠᏰᏟᏴ ᎤᎾᏗᏤᏁ ᎦᏚᎲ ᏂᎬᏫᏍᏕ ᏚᏂᎾᎡ ᏗᎪᏪᎳᏅ ᏗᏣᎳᎩ ᏗᎪᏪᎵ.

ᏧᎾᏕᏣᏝᏍᏗ ᏃᏊ ᏧᏓᎴᏅᎲᎠᏂᏲᏁᎦ ᎠᏂᏬᏂᏍᎩ ᏗᎾᏕᏲᎲᏍᎩ, ᎡᎵᏃ ᎪᎯᎩ ᏁᎲᎾ ᎢᎬᏤᎵᏍᏔᏅ ᎨᏎ ᏍᏏᏉᏯ ᏂᎬᏫᏍᏕᏃ ᏓᎾᏅᏓᏗᏍᎨ ᏣᎳᎩ ᏗᎪᏪᎳ. Ꮭ ᏳᏂᏲᏎᎴᎢ.

Now, who was this Sequoyah? my father asks.

He was a famous man, we say, because he invented writing for the Cherokee.

He was a brave man because he never gave up.

He was a leader because he showed his people how to survive—

How to stand tall and proud like these trees.

Ꮎ ᏍᎪᎠ Ᏽ ᎠᏗ ᎠꭳᏍꭰ ꭰᏏᎨꭰ ᏛᏙᏗ? ᏥᏙᏗ ᎠᎢᏲᏒ.

ᏛᎸᏃᏟ ᎠꭳᏍꭰ ᎥᏒ, ᏔᎸᎠꭰ, ᏂᎾᏍᏇꭰᏙᏃ ᏂꭳᏫ ᏛᏈᎹᎶᏝ

ᏣᎠꭳᏣᏙᏗ Ꭰꭰ ᏔᎾᏈᏇ ᎡᏇꭰ ᏺᎠꭳᏣᏗ ᏖᎡᎯ ᎢᏲꮁᏀᎦꭰᏗ.

ᏣᎸᏣꭰᏗ Ᏽ Ꮆ ᏍᏝᏝᎻꭰᎮᏔ.

ᏛᎸᏝᎯᎥᎠ ᏂꭳᏫ ᏍꭳᎮᏗ ᏔᏪꭳᎮᎯᏗ ᏅᎯᏍᎮᎦꭰᏗ ᎯᏍᎢᏔ.

ᏔᏂ ᏖᎸᎠ ᏟᎨᎠ ᎠᏗ ᏣᏍᎯᎦᏗ ᏍᎦᎡᏔ ᏂꭳᏫꭳᏔ. ᏫᏍᎯᎦᏝ.

a	e	i	o	u	v
ga ka	ge	gi	go	gu	gv
ha	he	hi	ho	hu	hv
la	le	li	lo	lu	lv
ma	me	mi	mo	mu	'v' is the sound of 'uh' in huh
na hna nah	ne	ni	no	nu	nv
qua	que	qui	quo	quu	quv
sa s	se	si	so	su	sv
da ta	de te	di ti	do	du	dv
dla tla	tle	tli	tlo	tlu	tlv
tsa	tse	tsi	tso	tsu	tsv
wa	we	wi	wo	wu	wv
ya	ye	yi	yo	yu	yv

ENGLISH SPEAKERS use an alphabet to spell out the sounds of a word. Cherokee speakers use a syllabary and write the syllables of a word. Take, for example, Sequoyah's daughter's name, Ayoka. It takes five English letters to write her name: a-y-o-k-a. But it takes only three Cherokee letters to do the same job: D-ꮂ-ꮼ. Spelling by syllables is not unique to Cherokee. About a billion and a half people—in India, Southeast Asia, Ethiopia, and Japan—use syllabaries.

SEQUOYAH'S GENIUS is rare. Only a handful of people in the last seven thousand years can claim to have invented a writing system. Sequoyah's system was not at all like ours. He did not invent an alphabet of twenty-six letters. He invented a syllabary of eighty-four signs, one for each syllable of the Cherokee language. Sequoyah's syllabary is still used today, and Sequoyah is honored as a hero not only of the Cherokee people but of our nation as well, for his statue stands in the U.S. Capitol building and his likeness graces the great bronze doors of the Library of Congress.

Sequoia* trees were first described in a scientific way by an Austrian man named Stephan Endlicher (1804–1849). When he died, scientists found his description of the tree along with a curious, hard-to-read name. Some thought the name was "Sequoyah"; others were not sure. How could a European know about a Cherokee man? It was unlikely, except for one thing—Endlicher was known to be interested in languages and writing systems from all over the world.

The story of Sequoyah's triumph has been told many times. Not every event in his life can be supported by facts. Often the facts compete with the legends that have arisen about this great man. It is for this reason I have used the phrases "they tell us" and "they say." To find out more about Sequoyah, read Grant Foreman's *Sequoyah* and Ruth Holmes and Betty Smith's account in their book *Beginning Cherokee*.

*It is customary today to have two spellings: *Sequoyah* for the man and *sequoia* for the tree.

Sequoyah

[also known as GEORGE GUESS OR GIST]

He was born between 1760 and 1765
in Monroe County, Tennessee,
the son of Wurteh of the Red Paint Clan
and Nathaniel Gist, a white trader.

◊

In 1809 or so, Sequoyah began working
on a writing system for the Cherokee language.

◊

After 1815, he moved near present-day
Sallisaw, Oklahoma, where his home still stands.

◊

In about 1821, he presented his ideas for a syllabary
to the Cherokee Nation.

◊

In 1828, the first newspaper printed in Cherokee,
called the *Phoenix*, was begun.
The *Phoenix* is still printed today.

◊

In 1843, Sequoyah died of old age and exhaustion
near San Fernando, Tamaulipas State, Mexico,
where he had gone to bring back
a band of refugee Cherokees.